RAFAEL NADAL'S
BOOK

How a Boy from Spain Became a
Legend in Tennis

Weedon KD

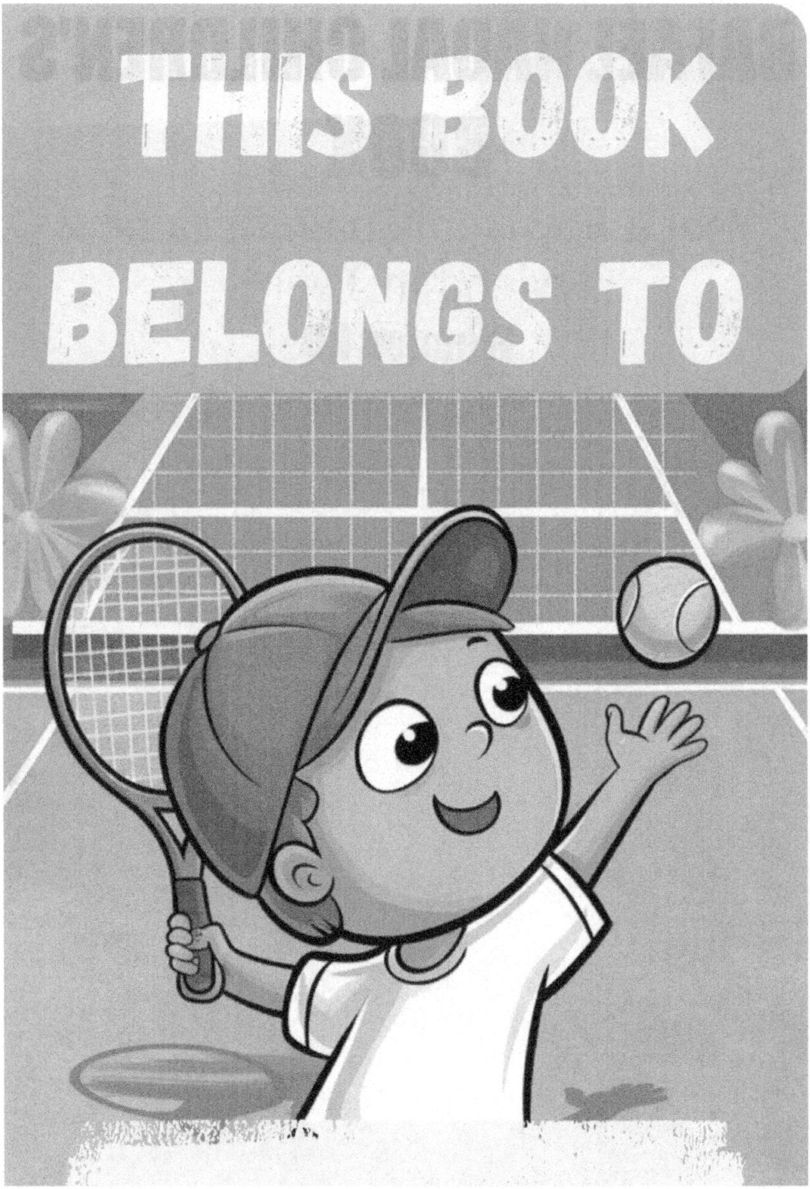
THIS BOOK
BELONGS TO

RAFAEL NADAL IS A FAMOUS TENNIS PLAYER FROM SPAIN, AND MANY PEOPLE BELIEVE HE'S ONE OF THE GREATEST TENNIS PLAYERS EVER!

IT TOOK YEARS OF PRACTICE, DEDICATION, AND A WHOLE LOT OF DETERMINATION. FROM THE TIME HE FIRST PICKED UP A TENNIS RACKET AS A THREE-YEAR-OLD,

TABLE OF CONTENTS

CHAPTER 1:Who is Rafael Nadal?..5
CHAPTER 2:Growing Up in Mallorca 5
CHAPTER 3:A Family of Athletes..5
CHAPTER 4:Early Tennis Dreams..5
CHAPTER 5:The First Big Win..5
CHAPTER 6:The King of Clay...5
CHAPTER 7:Challenges and Comebacks..5
CHAPTER 8:The Unstoppable Spirit...5
CHAPTER 9:Rafael's Grand Slam Journey 5
CHAPTER 10:Fun Facts About Rafael Nadal 5
CHAPTER 11:Words of Wisdom from Rafael 5
CHAPTER 12:Tennis Fun and Games...5
CHAPTER 13:Rafael's Legacy 5
Rafael Nadal Trivia Quiz..5
CONCLUSION 5
GLOSSARY 5
The Funny Tale of How Tennis Began 1

The Funny Tale of How Tennis Began

O nce upon a time, in a faraway kingdom called
Bounceville, people were always bored. The king, King
Boredom, had a huge problem: nobody knew how to have

fun! People would sit around all day doing nothing but staring at the clouds, and the kingdom was as quiet as a sleeping puppy. King Boredom scratched his head and said, "We need something exciting! But what?"

One day, a curious young boy named Timmy stumbled upon something strange while walking in the royal garden: an old, dusty box hidden under a tree. He opened it and found a strange wooden paddle and a small, fuzzy ball. "What's this?" Timmy asked. He tossed the ball into the air and hit it with the paddle. Boink! The ball bounced high into the air and landed on the other side of the garden. Timmy was amazed. "This could be fun!" he thought. He ran after the ball, hit it again, and watched it bounce over the garden fence. But then Timmy had an idea. "What if we make a game out of this?" he said, a grin spreading across his face.

Timmy raced to the castle and burst into the throne room. "Your Majesty, I've found something amazing!" he shouted, holding up the paddle and ball.

King Boredom yawned and looked at Timmy. "What's so amazing about a paddle and a fuzzy ball?" he asked.

"Watch this!" Timmy said. He tossed the ball into the air and hit it toward the king. The ball bounced off the king's crown, flew into the air, and landed right in the king's lap.

King Boredom blinked in surprise. "That was…fun!" he exclaimed. "What do you call this magical activity?"
"I don't know," said Timmy, scratching his head. "Maybe we can call it a Bounce Ball?"
The king thought for a moment. "Hmm, not catchy enough. How about something fancier, like… tennis?"
"Ten-nis? What's that supposed to mean?" Timmy asked.
The king shrugged. "I don't know. It just sounds royal and important!"
So, with a royal decree, King Boredom declared that from that day forward, the people of Bounceville would play tennis. But, of course, they needed rules. So the wise men of the court gathered around to create the rules:
You must hit the ball over a net (Timmy found an old fishing net in the castle's basement).
The ball must bounce within the court (King Boredom used chalk to draw a rectangle on the ground, though his lines were a bit wobbly).
You can't catch the ball with your hands! (This rule was added after the royal dog, Bouncy, kept catching the ball and running away with it).
The game quickly spread across the land. People were no longer bored, and King Boredom even changed his name

to King Excitement. The kingdom became lively, filled with the sound of bouncing tennis balls and laughter.

But that's not the end of the story! As the game grew, people started improving it. They made the paddles bigger and called them racquets. They invented different types of courts—like clay and grass—and gave funny names like "love" (because they loved playing so much) and "deuce" (which no one really understood, but it sounded cool).

And that, my friends, is how tennis was born. Thanks to a curious boy, a king who was tired of being bored, and a fuzzy ball, the world now has a game that millions of people play and enjoy every day!

The Moral of the Story:

Sometimes, great things start with a little curiosity, a bit of imagination, and a whole lot of fun. Keep exploring and trying new things—you never know what amazing ideas you might come up with!

CHAPTER 1:Who is Rafael Nadal?

Rafael Nadal is a famous tennis player from Spain, and many people believe he's one of the greatest tennis players ever! He was born on June 3, 1986, on the sunny island of

Mallorca, Spain. From a very young age, Rafael (or Rafa, as many people call him) loved playing sports. He tried soccer and even some other games, but his true passion was tennis.

Rafa is known for being super fast on the court and for never giving up, even when things get tough. He has won many important tennis competitions, called Grand Slam tournaments, especially on clay courts. In fact, he is so good at playing on clay that he earned the nickname "The King of Clay."

What makes Rafael Nadal one of the greatest players ever? It's his hard work, determination, and his amazing ability to come back from injuries stronger than ever. He has won 22 Grand Slam titles, including the French Open (which he has won 14 times!). That's a record!

So, when people think of tennis champions, Rafael Nadal always comes to mind because of his incredible skills, winning spirit, and love for the game!

CHAPTER 2:Growing Up in Mallorca

Rafael's Childhood on the Beautiful Island of Mallorca

Imagine growing up on a beautiful island surrounded by sparkling blue waters, sunny skies, and beaches where the sand feels warm under your feet. That's exactly what Rafael Nadal's childhood was like! He was born on June 3, 1986, on the sunny island of Mallorca, Spain. Mallorca is a magical place where you can swim in the sea, climb mountains, and explore nature. It's no wonder Rafael loved being outdoors!

As a little boy, Rafael—Rafa to his friends—was full of energy! He was always running, jumping, and playing with his cousins and friends. If you asked him what he liked to do, he'd probably say, "Everything!" Rafa loved all kinds of sports, especially soccer. In fact, he was so good at it that many people thought he'd become a soccer star. His uncle, Miguel Ángel Nadal, was even a professional soccer player, so sports ran in the family!

But guess what? Rafa had another uncle, Toni Nadal, who loved tennis. One day, Uncle Toni gave young Rafa a tennis racket, and that's where the real fun began. Little did anyone know, that simple racket would change Rafa's life forever!

First Steps on the Tennis Court

Rafa was only three years old when he picked up his first tennis racket. Can you imagine? He was so small that the racket probably looked huge in his tiny hands! At first, it was just a fun game for him, but Uncle Toni quickly saw something special in Rafa. Even though he was just a kid, Rafa was super focused and determined. Every time he hit the ball, he got better and better. Uncle Toni became his coach, and together, they spent hours practicing on the tennis courts of Mallorca.

But tennis wasn't the only thing on Rafa's mind. He still loved playing soccer with his friends, riding his bike around the island, and even swimming in the sea. Mallorca was like one big playground for him! When he wasn't practicing tennis, he was exploring the island, always on some kind of adventure.

Hard Work and Fun

Even though Rafa loved having fun, he learned something really important from his uncle: hard work. Uncle Toni didn't let Rafa slack off. He made sure Rafa practiced his tennis skills every day, no matter what. And guess what? Rafa didn't mind! He loved the challenge of trying to get better. Whether it was hot and sunny or windy and cold, Rafa showed up to practice with a smile on his face, ready to play.

At school, Rafa was just like other kids. He had homework, friends, and loved playing with his toys. But what made him different was his incredible focus and his love for the game. Whenever he was on the tennis court, he gave it his all. He didn't just hit the ball—he chased it down with lightning speed and hit it as hard as he could. Even as a kid, you could tell Rafa had something special.

Tennis, Family, and Friends

Even though Rafa was training to be a tennis champion, his family made sure he had time to be a regular kid. His parents, Sebastià and Ana María, were always there to support him. Rafa's family was very close, and they made sure he stayed grounded and humble, no matter how good he became at tennis. His sister, María Isabel, also cheered him on and kept him company during those long practice sessions.

When Rafa wasn't practicing, he spent time playing with his friends. They would ride bikes, play soccer, and sometimes even play a little tennis together. Rafa always made sure to have fun, even while working hard to improve his skills.

A Star in the Making

By the time Rafa was eight years old, he had already won his first tennis tournament! Can you believe it? At such a young age, Rafa was already showing the world that he was a tennis star in the making. Even though he was winning trophies, Rafa didn't let it go to his head. He stayed humble and kept practicing every day. After all, he wasn't just playing tennis for fame—he was playing because he loved the game.

So, while other kids were dreaming of becoming astronauts, doctors, or superheroes, little Rafa was busy on the tennis court, perfecting his serve and chasing down every ball. And even though he didn't know it yet, the boy from the beautiful island of Mallorca was on his way to becoming one of the greatest tennis players the world had ever seen.

In Mallorca, Rafa found the perfect place to grow, explore, and practice. Surrounded by nature, sunshine, and his loving family, he discovered his passion for tennis. And as we now know, that passion would soon take him far beyond the island's shores, to tennis courts all over the world!

CHAPTER 3:A Family of Athletes

How Rafael Nadal's Family Helped Shape His Love for Sports

Rafael Nadal's family played a huge role in shaping his love for sports and supporting his dream of becoming a tennis champion. From the very beginning, Rafa's family was there to cheer him on, give him advice, and encourage him to follow his dreams. Let's find out how they influenced his journey to becoming one of the greatest tennis players ever!

A Sports-Loving Family

Rafa grew up in a family that loved sports! His uncle, Miguel Ángel Nadal, was a famous soccer player who played for FC Barcelona and the Spanish national team. Rafa loved watching his uncle play and even thought about becoming a soccer star himself. But sports wasn't just something his uncle enjoyed—Rafa's whole family loved it. They would gather together to watch big soccer matches and other sporting events, so it was no surprise that young Rafa caught the sports bug early on.

But it wasn't just soccer that got Rafa excited. His other uncle, Toni Nadal, was a big tennis fan, and he was the one who introduced Rafa to tennis. Toni quickly noticed that Rafa had a special talent for the game. He saw that even as a little boy, Rafa was incredibly determined, focused, and eager to learn. So, when Rafa was only three years old,

Uncle Toni started coaching him in tennis, helping him develop his skills.

Uncle Toni: The Coach and Mentor

Uncle Toni wasn't just a regular coach—he was also Rafa's mentor. He believed in tough training sessions and discipline, always pushing Rafa to do his best. Uncle Toni taught Rafa the importance of hard work, humility, and never giving up, even when things got tough. He also taught Rafa to be mentally strong and never let fear or frustration get the best of him. These lessons would stay with Rafa for his entire career.

But don't worry! Even though Uncle Toni was strict, he and Rafa had a lot of fun on the court, too. They laughed, joked, and enjoyed the game together. Uncle Toni knew that while hard work was important, enjoying the sport was just as crucial.

Thanks to Uncle Tony's guidance and encouragement, Rafa became more and more skilled at tennis. The bond they shared was special, and together they would work hard, with Rafa's family always cheering them on.

Rafa's Parents: Support and Encouragement

Rafa's parents, Sebastià and Ana María, were his biggest supporters from the start. They knew how much Rafa loved sports, and they encouraged him to follow his passion. But they also made sure he had balance in his life. They wanted Rafa to enjoy his childhood, spend time with friends, and focus on his studies at school, too.

Rafa's parents never pushed him too hard; instead, they supported him in whatever he wanted to do. If he wanted to play tennis, they would take him to practice and tournaments. If he wanted to play soccer with his friends, they made sure he had time for that, too. His parents always believed that having fun was just as important as working hard, and they helped Rafa stay grounded and humble.

His family taught him important values like respect, kindness, and patience. Rafa's parents wanted him to grow up to be not just a great athlete, but also a great person. They believed in the power of hard work, but they also wanted Rafa to be happy and well-rounded.

His Sister: A Constant Cheerleader

Rafa's younger sister, María Isabel, was also a big part of his support system. Even though she didn't play tennis, she was always there to cheer him on. Whether Rafa was playing in a local match or a big tournament, María Isabel was always proud of her big brother. They were very close and often spent time together as a family, going on outings and sharing laughs.

Having such a strong, loving family helped Rafa stay motivated and positive, even during tough times. He knew that no matter what happened on the tennis court, his family would always be there for him, supporting him every step of the way.

Family Values: Humility and Hard Work

One of the things that made Rafa stand out, even as a young boy, was his humility. Despite winning tennis matches and gaining attention, Rafa never acted like he was better than anyone else. This humility came from his family. They always reminded him to stay grounded and to never let success go to his head. His family believed that staying humble was just as important as winning trophies. Even as Rafa became a tennis superstar, his family made sure he remembered the values he learned growing up: hard work, respect, and kindness. Rafa's family taught him that being a champion wasn't just about winning on the court—it was also about being a good person off the court.

A Dream Come True

Thanks to his family's influence, Rafa developed a deep love for sports and the determination to become the best tennis player he could be. From his uncle Toni's coaching, to his parents' encouragement, to his sister's support, Rafa had an amazing team behind him, helping him chase his dream.

And what's even better? Rafa never forgot the lessons his family taught him. Even as he became one of the greatest tennis players in the world, Rafa always remained humble, hardworking, and grateful for the love and support of his family.

So, if you ever dream of achieving something big, just remember that, like Rafael Nadal, having a strong and loving family by your side can help make that dream come true!

CHAPTER 4:Early Tennis Dreams

Rafael's First Steps Into the World of Tennis

Rafael Nadal's journey into the world of tennis began when he was just a little boy, and from the very first time he picked up a racket, it was clear that he had a special talent. But more than just talent, it was his determination and hard work that set him apart.

A Young Boy with a Big Dream

Rafa was only three years old when his uncle, Toni Nadal, first introduced him to tennis. At that age, most kids are just learning how to ride a bike, but Rafa was already swinging a tennis racket! His uncle Toni had a passion for the game and saw that Rafa had the potential to be great. So, they began practicing together.

At first, Rafa was just a little boy with big energy, running around the court and hitting balls with all his might. But even at such a young age, he showed incredible focus. While many kids might get distracted or bored, Rafa loved every second of it. He wanted to keep playing, keep practicing, and keep getting better.

Hard Work from the Start

As Rafa grew older, his love for tennis only deepened. Uncle Toni became his coach, and they trained together regularly. But Uncle Toni didn't take it easy on Rafa just because he was family. In fact, he was strict and made sure that Rafa worked hard, no matter how talented he was.

Rafa practiced for hours each day, learning all the important skills of tennis: how to serve, how to volley, how to hit the ball with power and precision. He didn't mind the hard work. In fact, he loved it. He was determined to improve, no matter how many hours it took.

Uncle Toni also taught Rafa about the mental side of tennis. He made sure Rafa understood that being a champion wasn't just about having fast feet or a strong arm—it was also about having a strong mind. Rafa learned to stay calm, focused, and never give up, even when a match was tough.

Early Competitions

By the time Rafa was just eight years old, he started entering local tennis competitions. These were small tournaments, but for Rafa, they were a chance to test everything he had been learning. And guess what? He won his very first tournament!

Winning his first tennis tournament was a big moment for young Rafa. It made him realize that all the hard work was paying off. But instead of celebrating too much, Rafa went straight back to the tennis court, ready to practice even harder. He didn't want to just be good—he wanted to be the best!

Balancing Tennis with Fun

Even though Rafa was serious about tennis, he didn't stop being a kid. When he wasn't practicing, he still found time to play soccer with his friends, ride his bike, and have fun on the beautiful island of Mallorca. His family made sure he had a balanced life, full of laughter and play, even while he was training to be a tennis star.

But every time he stepped onto the tennis court, Rafa switched into competition mode. He listened to his uncle's advice, studied his mistakes, and worked on becoming stronger and faster. He was never satisfied with being "just okay." Rafa wanted to be great, and he knew that greatness only came through practice and determination.

Never Giving Up

Rafa's determination is what truly made him stand out. Tennis can be a very challenging sport, both physically and mentally. Players need to be fast, strong, and think quickly. There were times when Rafa lost matches or struggled during tough games. But one thing Rafa was known for, even as a young player, was his never-give-up attitude.

Even when he was losing, Rafa kept fighting for every point. He didn't let frustration or disappointment get to him. Instead, he used it as motivation to get better. He believed that with hard work, he could always improve. This determination became one of Rafa's greatest strengths and would help him win many matches in the future.

A Future Star in the Making

By the time Rafa was in his early teens, he was already playing in bigger tournaments, facing older and more experienced players. Some people might have been nervous, but not Rafa. He thrived on the challenge. He wasn't afraid to compete against the best, and with each match, he gained more confidence and experience.

Rafa's first steps into the world of tennis were full of hard work, fun, and an unshakeable belief in himself. His family, especially Uncle Toni, helped guide him, but it was Rafa's own determination that pushed him forward. He knew that becoming a champion wasn't something that happened overnight. It took years of practice, sweat, and focus.

From his very first swing of the racket, Rafael Nadal showed that he wasn't just any ordinary kid. He was a future tennis star, ready to take on the world. And with his determination to succeed, it wasn't long before he started making his mark in the sport he loved so much!

CHAPTER 5:The First Big Win

Rafael's Journey as a Young Tennis Player and His First Major Victory

Rafael Nadal's journey to tennis greatness didn't happen overnight. It took years of practice, dedication, and a whole lot of determination. From the time he first picked up a tennis racket as a three-year-old, Rafa worked hard to improve every single day. Let's follow Rafa's exciting journey as a young tennis player and how he claimed his first major victory on the court!

A Tennis Prodigy in the Making

By the time Rafa was in his early teens, it was clear to everyone that he had a special talent for tennis. He was playing in local tournaments, and even though he was still young, he often beat older, more experienced players. Rafa wasn't just good; he was determined. He had a fierce fighting spirit and never gave up, no matter how tough the competition got.

As Rafa grew older, his uncle Toni continued to train him, pushing him to be the best he could be. Rafa's skills improved rapidly, and he started competing in junior tournaments around Spain and Europe. He loved the thrill of competition and the chance to challenge himself against other talented young players.

First Major Victory: The Spanish Championships

When Rafa was 14 years old, he had his first taste of major success. He entered the Spanish National Championships, a big tournament for junior players in Spain. Rafa knew this was a chance to prove himself and show just how far he had come.

The competition was tough. Rafa faced some of the best young tennis players in the country, and every match was a challenge. But Rafa wasn't one to back down from a challenge. With his strong forehand, powerful serves, and incredible speed, he fought hard in every game.

Rafa's biggest strength, though, wasn't just his physical ability—it was his mental toughness. Even when the matches were close, and the pressure was high, Rafa stayed calm and focused. He believed in himself and knew that all the hard work he had put in was about to pay off.

In the final match of the Spanish Championships, Rafa faced his toughest opponent yet. The match was intense, with both players giving it their all. But Rafa's determination shone through, and after an epic battle on the court, Rafa emerged victorious. He had won his first major championship!

The Moment of Triumph

Winning the Spanish National Championships was a huge moment for young Rafa. It was his first major victory, and it showed the world that he was a rising star in the world of tennis. But for Rafa, this win wasn't just about the trophy or the title. It was about proving to himself that he could achieve his dreams through hard work and dedication.

When the final point was won, Rafa was filled with joy. His family and Uncle Toni were there to celebrate with him, and they were all incredibly proud. But even after winning such a big tournament, Rafa didn't let it go to his head. He stayed humble, knowing that this was just the beginning of his journey.

Building Confidence for the Future

This victory gave Rafa the confidence to keep pushing forward. He knew that if he could win a major championship at just 14 years old, there were no limits to what he could achieve. Rafa continued to train hard, working on his weaknesses and improving his strengths. But what made Rafa special wasn't just his talent. It was his incredible work ethic and his desire to keep learning. Even after winning, Rafa never stopped trying to improve. He was always looking for ways to get better, always pushing himself to reach new heights.

A Taste of What Was to Come

Rafa's first major victory was a glimpse of what was to come. He was already being recognized as one of the best young tennis players in Spain, but this win put him on the path to international success. It wasn't long before he started competing in bigger tournaments around the world, going up against the best junior players from other countries.

And while Rafa would go on to win many more titles and championships in the future, his first major victory on the tennis court would always be special. It was a reminder of how far he had come, from a little boy with a big dream to a tennis champion in the making.

The Future Star

Rafa's journey as a young tennis player was full of challenges, hard work, and exciting victories. He had proven that with determination and perseverance, anything was possible. His first major victory was just the beginning of a legendary career that would see him become one of the greatest tennis players the world had ever seen.

But no matter how many titles Rafa would win in the years to come, he would never forget those early days—his first steps onto the tennis court, the lessons from Uncle Toni, and the joy of winning his first big tournament. It was the foundation of his journey, a journey that would take him to the top of the tennis world!

CHAPTER 6:The King of Clay

Why Rafael Nadal is Called the "King of Clay" and How
He Mastered the French Open

Do you know why Rafael Nadal is called the "King of
Clay"? Well, get ready to find out, because this is a story
about determination, hard work, and a love for tennis that
made Rafa one of the greatest players ever on clay courts!

What's So Special About Clay Courts?

First, let's talk about what a clay court is. Tennis can be
played on different types of surfaces, like grass, hard
courts, or clay. Clay courts are made from crushed brick,
and they're a little slower than other surfaces. The ball
bounces differently on clay, making it tricky to play on.
Clay courts demand a lot of skill. You need to be quick on
your feet, slide around, and have a special kind of patience
to win. And guess what? Rafa became a master at playing
on this tough surface!

Rafa's Secret to Success on Clay

So how did Rafa become the "King of Clay"? It all started
with his unique playing style. On clay, Rafa is known for
his incredible footwork and his ability to hit the ball with

spin. He has a special way of making the ball bounce high and fast, which makes it really hard for his opponents to return the ball.

But it's not just about technique. Rafa is known for his never-give-up attitude. On clay courts, where matches can last for hours, Rafa is always ready for a long fight. He's like a superhero who doesn't get tired! He runs down every ball, slides across the court, and keeps hitting powerful shots until his opponent gives up.

Rafa's mental toughness on clay is legendary. He stays calm under pressure, focuses on every point, and doesn't let anything stop him. That's why he's won so many matches on this surface—he's not just strong physically, but mentally too!

The French Open: Rafa's Favorite Tournament

Now, let's talk about the French Open, one of the biggest and most famous tennis tournaments in the world. The French Open is played on clay, which is perfect for Rafa. Every year, tennis players from all over the world come to Paris, France, to compete in this amazing tournament. And Rafa? Well, he's made it his playground!

Rafa played his very first French Open in 2005, when he was only 19 years old. Most players don't win a Grand Slam (a super important tennis tournament) on their first try, but Rafa isn't like most players. He won his very first French Open that year! It was an incredible victory, and from that moment on, people started noticing that Rafa was something special on clay.

Dominating the French Open

But Rafa didn't just win once. Year after year, Rafa kept coming back to the French Open, and year after year, he kept winning. He was so good on the clay courts in Paris that he started to seem unstoppable. Rafa's opponents would try their best, but it was almost like he had superpowers whenever he stepped onto the clay at the French Open.

By the time Rafa won his 14th French Open title in 2022, he had set a record that no one had ever seen before. No other player in tennis history has won a single Grand Slam tournament as many times as Rafa has won the French Open. That's why people started calling him the "King of Clay"—because no one else can play on clay like Rafa can!

Rafa's Amazing French Open Wins

Every time Rafa wins the French Open, it's like watching a master artist at work. He slides across the clay like he's skating, hitting powerful shots from every corner of the court. The crowd goes wild, cheering for every point, and Rafa just keeps going, determined to win.

Here's a cool fact: at the French Open, there's a special trophy called the Musketeers' Cup that the winner gets to hold. Rafa has lifted that trophy 14 times, each time with a big smile on his face. He knows how hard he worked to win it, and he's proud of every victory.

What Makes Rafa the "King of Clay"?

So, why is Rafa called the "King of Clay"? It's because of his incredible record at the French Open and his unmatched skill on clay courts. He's won more titles on clay than anyone else in the history of tennis. But it's not just about the wins. Rafa's nickname comes from his dedication, his passion for the game, and the way he never gives up, even when the matches get tough.

And remember, Rafa didn't become the "King of Clay" overnight. It took years of practice, hard work, and believing in himself. He showed the world that with determination and grit, you can achieve incredible things—even become the best player on a challenging surface like clay!

Rafa's Message for You

Rafa's journey on clay is a great reminder that success isn't always easy, but if you work hard and stay focused, you can achieve your dreams. Whether it's in tennis, school, or anything else you love to do, Rafa's story shows that with enough practice and heart, you can be the best version of yourself.

So, next time you watch a tennis match on TV or play a game of tennis with your friends, remember the story of Rafael Nadal, the "King of Clay," who mastered the French Open with his unstoppable spirit!

CHAPTER 7:Challenges and Comebacks

Discover the Challenges Rafael Faced and How He Always Came Back

Rafael Nadal's journey to becoming one of the greatest tennis players of all time wasn't all smooth sailing. Along the way, he faced many challenges, including injuries that might have stopped other players. But what makes Rafa so special is how he always came back stronger than ever. Let's dive into the obstacles Rafa faced and how he turned them into opportunities for an incredible comeback!

The Challenge of Injuries

Even the best athletes face injuries, and Rafa's career was no exception. Throughout his time as a tennis star, he experienced several injuries that tested his resilience and determination. But Rafa didn't let these setbacks stop him. Instead, he used them as motivation to work even harder.

Knee Problems: One of the first major challenges Rafa faced was trouble with his knees. Tennis involves a lot of running, jumping, and quick movements, which can be really tough on the knees. Rafa had to deal with pain and discomfort, especially on the hard courts. He needed to take breaks and adjust his training to make sure he didn't hurt himself more.

Wrist Injuries: Another significant challenge came in the form of wrist injuries. Rafa's powerful game meant that his wrists took a lot of strain. He had to carefully manage his training and sometimes even take breaks from playing to let his wrist heal. This was tough for someone as passionate about tennis as Rafa.

Abdominal Issues: Rafa also faced issues with his abdomen. Tennis players often need to use their core muscles a lot, and injuries in this area can be particularly troublesome. Rafa had to adjust his playstyle and focus on healing before he could return to his best form.

How Rafa Overcome These Challenges

Even though injuries could be really discouraging, Rafa never let them keep him down for long. Here's how he managed to overcome these obstacles:

Strong Work Ethic: Rafa's incredible work ethic played a crucial role in his comebacks. Even when he was injured, he would work with doctors, physiotherapists, and trainers to make sure he was recovering properly. He followed his rehab plans with dedication and made sure to stay as fit as possible, even when he couldn't play.

Mental Toughness: Rafa's mental toughness was another key factor in his comebacks. He always stayed positive and focused on his goals. He knew that every challenge was a chance to learn and grow. This positive mindset helped him stay motivated and ready to return to the court.

Adapting His Game: When Rafa came back from injuries, he sometimes had to adjust his game to protect his body. For example, he might have changed his training routines or modified his playing style slightly to reduce the strain on his injured areas. This adaptability helped him continue performing at a high level despite his challenges.

Support from Family and Team: Throughout his career, Rafa had strong support from his family and his team. They encouraged him during tough times and celebrated his successes. This support was incredibly important for Rafa's recovery and helped him stay determined.

The Joy of the Comeback

One of the most inspiring things about Rafa is how he celebrated his comebacks. Every time he returned from an injury, he came back with even more determination and passion. His fans were always excited to see him back on the court, and Rafa's performances were often filled with the same energy and brilliance as before.

For instance, after a significant injury break, Rafa made a triumphant return to win the 2013 French Open, proving once again that he was a force to be reckoned with. Each comeback was a testament to his hard work, resilience, and love for the game.

The Lesson of Resilience

Rafa's journey teaches us an important lesson: even when you face setbacks or challenges, it's possible to come back stronger than ever. His story shows that with hard work, determination, and the right mindset, you can overcome obstacles and achieve your dreams.

So, next time you face a challenge, remember Rafael Nadal's amazing ability to bounce back from injuries and setbacks. Like Rafa, you can use challenges as opportunities to learn, grow, and come back even better!

Rafa's ability to keep going, no matter what, is a big part of why he's known as one of the greatest tennis players ever. His story is a true inspiration, showing that with enough perseverance and a positive attitude, anything is possible.

CHAPTER 8:The Unstoppable Spirit

Rafael Nadal's Never-Give-Up Attitude and How He Inspires Young Athletes Everywhere

Rafael Nadal is more than just a tennis superstar; he's known for his never-give-up attitude. His resilience, determination, and relentless spirit have made him a role model for young athletes all over the world. Let's explore how Rafa's incredible attitude inspires and motivates, and why his story is so powerful.

The Heart of a Fighter

From the beginning of his career, Rafael Nadal has been famous for his fighting spirit on the tennis court. No matter how tough the match or how far behind he might be, Rafa never gives up. He battles for every point with an energy and enthusiasm that is truly amazing.

Fighting Through Tough Matches: Rafa's never-give-up attitude is especially evident in long and difficult matches. He's known for his ability to come back from behind, even when it looks like he might lose. In one memorable match at the 2012 Australian Open, Rafa fought through a grueling five-set battle that lasted over five hours. Even when he was tired and facing strong opponents, he kept pushing forward, showing that he would never surrender. Overcoming Injuries: Rafa's attitude shines brightly when he's recovering from injuries. Despite the frustration of having to take breaks from playing, he remains positive and focused on his recovery. He sees injuries not as obstacles, but as opportunities to become even stronger. His determination to come back and compete at the highest level, despite the setbacks, inspires everyone to keep going, no matter what challenges they face.

Inspiring Young Athletes

Rafa's never-give-up attitude has made him a hero for young athletes everywhere. Kids who look up to him see more than just a tennis champion—they see someone who embodies perseverance and dedication.

Hard Work and Discipline: Rafa's commitment to his sport is a lesson in hard work and discipline. He practices tirelessly, always looking for ways to improve his game.

Young athletes can learn from Rafa's example that success comes from putting in the effort, practicing regularly, and never cutting corners.

Positive Attitude: Rafa's positive attitude, even in the face of difficulties, is incredibly inspiring. He always maintains a smile and a respectful demeanor, no matter the outcome of the match. This positivity teaches young athletes that having a good attitude, even when things aren't going perfectly, is just as important as being skilled.

Respect for the Game: Rafa's respect for tennis, his opponents, and the fans is a big part of why he's admired. He plays with integrity and shows sportsmanship, treating everyone involved with kindness and respect. This behavior sets a powerful example for young people about how to be gracious winners and humble losers.

Balancing Life: Even with his busy schedule, Rafa makes time for his family and friends. He shows young athletes that while pursuing their dreams is important, maintaining a balance and cherishing relationships is equally valuable.

Real-Life Impact

Many young athletes have been inspired by Rafael Nadal's story. Coaches and parents often use his achievements and attitude as examples to motivate kids to work hard and stay determined. Schools and sports programs may highlight

Rafa's perseverance to teach students the value of persistence and resilience.

A Lasting Legacy

Rafa's never-give-up attitude isn't just about winning trophies. It's about his approach to life and sports—a commitment to doing his best, regardless of the circumstances. His story teaches that true greatness is achieved not only through victories but also through overcoming obstacles and showing unwavering resolve.

For every young athlete who dreams of achieving greatness, Rafael Nadal's example is a guiding light. His journey shows that with determination, hard work, and a positive attitude, anything is possible. Rafa's impact extends beyond tennis; he inspires kids everywhere to believe in themselves, work hard, and never give up on their dreams.

CHAPTER 9:Rafael's Grand Slam Journey

Rafael Nadal's Path to Winning Multiple Grand Slam Titles and What Makes Him So Special in Tennis
Rafael Nadal's journey to becoming one of the greatest tennis players of all time is marked by his incredible

achievements, especially his impressive record in Grand Slam tournaments. His success on the court isn't just about the number of titles he's won but also about what makes him truly special in the world of tennis. Let's explore his path to Grand Slam glory and the unique qualities that set him apart.

The Grand Slam Journey

Grand Slam tournaments are the biggest and most prestigious events in tennis. There are four of them each year:

The Australian Open (January)

The French Open (May-June)

Wimbledon (June-July)

The US Open (August-September)

Winning these tournaments is a major achievement for any player, and Rafael Nadal has excelled in all of them.

Early Success: Rafa's Grand Slam journey began with a remarkable victory at the 2005 French Open. At just 19 years old, he won his first major title, showcasing his talent and resilience. This win was the start of what would become a legendary career.

Mastering the Clay: The French Open is played on clay courts, and Nadal quickly became known as the "King of Clay." His dominance on this surface has led him to win the French Open 14 times, a record no other player has matched. His powerful groundstrokes, incredible footwork, and ability to play long rallies make him unbeatable on clay.

Winning on Other Surfaces: While Rafa is best known for his clay court success, he has also achieved greatness on other surfaces. He has won two Australian Open titles, two Wimbledon titles, and four US Open titles. This versatility shows that he can adapt his game to different conditions, a key factor in his Grand Slam success.

Comeback Victories: Throughout his career, Rafa has faced challenges like injuries and tough competition. But each time he came back, he did so with even more determination. His victories after comebacks, such as his win at the 2013 French Open following a period of injuries, are testaments to his incredible resilience and skill.

What Makes Rafael Nadal Special

Rafa's success in tennis is due to a combination of unique qualities and attributes:

Unmatched Work Ethic: Rafa's dedication to the sport is legendary. He trains tirelessly, always looking for ways to improve. His work ethic sets him apart from many other players and contributes to his success on the court.

Exceptional Physical Fitness: Tennis is a physically demanding sport, and Rafa's fitness is one of his greatest assets. His agility, strength, and endurance allow him to compete at the highest level and handle the physical challenges of long matches and tough opponents.

Mental Toughness: Rafa's mental strength is one of his most remarkable qualities. He stays calm under pressure, maintains focus during intense moments, and never lets setbacks or difficulties affect his performance. This mental toughness helps him stay competitive and win crucial points.

Strategic Play: Rafa's ability to strategize and adapt his playstyle is another key to his success. He reads the game exceptionally well and adjusts his tactics based on his opponent's strengths and weaknesses. His use of spin, especially on clay, is a crucial part of his game.

Sportsmanship and Humility: Despite his success, Rafa is known for his sportsmanship and humility. He treats his opponents with respect and handles both victories and losses gracefully. His attitude off the court makes him a beloved figure in the tennis world.

Passion for the Game: Above all, Rafael Nadal's passion for tennis shines through. He loves the sport and plays with incredible enthusiasm and joy. This love for the game fuels his drive and keeps him motivated to continue competing at the highest level.

The Legacy of Rafael Nadal

Rafa's path to winning multiple Grand Slam titles and his unique qualities make him a true legend in tennis. His success is not just about the trophies but also about the way he plays the game—with dedication, resilience, and a deep love for tennis.

For young athletes and fans alike, Rafael Nadal's story is an inspiration. His journey teaches that with hard work, determination, and a positive attitude, it's possible to achieve great things. Rafa's legacy in tennis is a testament to the power of passion and perseverance in reaching the top of one's sport.

CHAPTER 10:Fun Facts About Rafael Nadal

Cool and Interesting Facts About Rafael Nadal

Rafael Nadal is not only a tennis legend but also a person with some pretty cool and interesting hobbies and interests outside of the sport. Let's dive into some fun facts about Rafa that you might not know!

Fun Facts About Rafael Nadal

Born to Play: Rafael Nadal was born on June 3, 1986, in Manacor, Mallorca, Spain. He was introduced to sports at a young age by his uncle Toni Nadal, who was also his coach. Rafa's family has always been deeply involved in sports, and his early exposure helped shape his incredible tennis career.

Tennis is in His Blood: Rafa comes from a sporty family. His uncle Miguel Angel Nadal was a professional soccer player, and his father, Sebastian Nadal, has been involved in various sports, including tennis. The love for sports runs deep in the Nadal family!

A Fan of Football: When he's not on the tennis court, Rafa enjoys watching and playing football (soccer). He's a big fan of the local team, RCD Mallorca, and often attends their matches. Football is one of his favorite sports to watch and play in his free time.

Passionate About Charity: Rafael Nadal is known for his charitable work. He founded the Rafael Nadal Foundation, which focuses on providing educational and sports opportunities to disadvantaged children. Rafa's foundation helps kids achieve their dreams through sports and education, reflecting his commitment to giving back to the community.

A Big Family Guy: Family is very important to Rafa. He has a close relationship with his parents and sister, María Isabel Nadal. They often travel with him and support him during tournaments. Rafa's family bond is a big part of his life and success.

Loves to Relax with Fishing: When he's looking to relax and unwind, Rafa enjoys fishing. It's a peaceful activity that helps him take a break from the intense training and competition. Fishing allows him to enjoy the calmness of nature and spend quality time away from the tennis court.

A Fan of Spanish Cuisine: Rafa loves Spanish food, especially dishes like paella and seafood. He enjoys sharing meals with his family and friends, and he has a soft spot for traditional Spanish dishes. Food is a big part of his cultural heritage and personal enjoyment.

Injuries and Fashion: Rafa is known for his distinctive style on the tennis court, including his trademark sleeveless shirts. This look was partly due to his desire to be comfortable and also because of his ongoing battle with injuries. His fashion choices often reflect his personal comfort and practical needs.

A Polite and Humble Hero: Despite his fame and success, Rafa is known for his humility and sportsmanship. He treats everyone with kindness and respect, whether it's opponents, fans, or teammates. His positive attitude and respectful behavior make him a beloved figure both on and off the court.

A Lover of Nature: Rafa enjoys spending time in nature, especially in his hometown of Mallorca. The beautiful landscapes and natural surroundings of the island are close to his heart. He often takes time to appreciate the outdoors and relax in the natural beauty of his home.

Rafael Nadal's interests and passions outside of tennis show that he's a well-rounded individual with a love for family, charity, and relaxation. His dedication to both his sport and his personal interests makes him a fascinating and inspiring figure. Whether on the court or off, Rafa's cool and interesting facts add to his impressive and beloved persona.

CHAPTER 11:Words of Wisdom from Rafael

Rafael Nadal's Advice on Working Hard, Staying Humble, and Following Your Dreams

Rafael Nadal, one of the greatest tennis players of all time, has not only achieved tremendous success but also shares valuable life lessons with young people everywhere. His advice on working hard, staying humble, and following your dreams comes from his own experiences and journey. Let's hear what Rafa has to say about these important aspects of life.

1. Working Hard

Rafael Nadal believes that hard work is the key to achieving your goals. He often talks about how dedication and effort are crucial to success in any field. Here's what he advises:

Commit Fully: Rafa says that to reach your goals, you need to be fully committed. This means putting in the effort every single day, whether it's practicing tennis, studying for school, or working on a project. Consistency and dedication are essential.

Embrace Challenges: According to Rafa, challenges are a natural part of the journey. Instead of avoiding them, face them head-on. Each challenge you overcome helps you grow and get closer to your goals. He often reflects on how he worked through injuries and tough matches to continue improving.

Stay Focused: Rafa advises young people to stay focused on their objectives. It's easy to get distracted, but keeping your eyes on the prize and working diligently will help you achieve your dreams.

2. Staying Humble

Despite his success, Rafael Nadal is known for his humility. He believes that staying humble is crucial, regardless of how successful you become. Here's his perspective on humility:

Appreciate Others: Rafa emphasizes the importance of respecting and appreciating others, including your competitors. He often mentions how he learns from his opponents and values the contributions of his team and family.

Be Grateful: Rafa advises to always be grateful for the opportunities you have and the support you receive. Recognizing the help and encouragement from others keeps you grounded and focused on what truly matters.

Stay True to Yourself: He encourages people to remain true to who they are, no matter how much success they achieve. Maintaining your values and being authentic helps you stay humble and connected to your roots.

3. Following Your Dreams

Rafa's journey to becoming a tennis champion is a testament to the power of following your dreams. Here's his advice on pursuing your passions:

Believe in Yourself: Rafa stresses the importance of self-belief. He believes that if you have a dream, you should trust in your abilities and work towards it. Even when faced with setbacks, believing in yourself helps you keep going.

Pursue What You Love: He advises finding something you are passionate about and pursuing it wholeheartedly. When you love what you do, it makes the hard work and effort feel worthwhile.

Be Patient and Persistent: Success doesn't come overnight. Rafa encourages young people to be patient and persistent in their efforts. The journey towards achieving your dreams is often long and challenging, but staying committed will eventually lead to success.

Enjoy the Journey: Lastly, Rafa reminds us to enjoy the journey towards our goals. While working hard is important, it's equally important to find joy in what you're doing and appreciate the experiences along the way.

Rafael Nadal's advice on working hard, staying humble, and following your dreams comes from his own experiences and the values he holds dear. His journey teaches us that with dedication, respect, and a passion for what you do, you can achieve great things and inspire others along the way.

CHAPTER 12:Tennis Fun and Games

Fun Activities: Quiz and Tennis Challenges!

Get ready to dive into some fun activities to learn more about Rafael Nadal and test your tennis skills right at home! Here is a quiz about Rafa's career and some tennis challenges you can try.

Rafael Nadal Quiz

Test your knowledge about Rafael Nadal with this fun quiz!

When was Rafael Nadal born?

A) June 3, 1986

B) July 4, 1987

C) May 15, 1985

D) August 1, 1986

How many times has Rafael Nadal won the French Open as of 2024?

A) 12

B) 14

C) 16

D) 18

Which surface is Rafael Nadal famously known for dominating?

A) Grass

B) Hard Court

C) Clay

D) Carpet

What is Rafael Nadal's nickname?

A) The King of Grass

B) The Spanish Sensation

C) The King of Clay

D) The Master of Hard Courts

Which Grand Slam did Rafael Nadal win first?

A) Wimbledon

B) The US Open

C) The Australian Open

D) The French Open

What sport does Rafael Nadal enjoy playing in addition to tennis?

A) Basketball

B) Soccer (Football)

C) Baseball

D) Golf

What is the name of Rafael Nadal's charity foundation?

A) Rafa Nadal Foundation

B) Nadal's Heroes

C) Rafa's Charitable Trust

D) Nadal Kids Foundation

Which country is Rafael Nadal from?

A) Spain

B) France

C) Italy

D) Portugal

Answers:

A) June 3, 1986

B) 14

C) Clay

C) The King of Clay

D) The French Open

B) Soccer (Football)

A) Rafa Nadal Foundation

A) Spain

Tennis Challenges to Try at Home

Wall Rally Challenge:

Find a clear wall and a tennis ball. Stand a few feet away and hit the ball against the wall, trying to keep a rally going. Count how many hits you can make in a row without the ball touching the ground. Try to beat your own record!

Serve Practice:

Set up a target area on the ground (you can use a hula hoop or a piece of tape). Practice serving the ball into the target area. See how many times you can hit the target in a row. Try to improve your accuracy with each serve.

Footwork Fun:

Tennis players need quick feet. Create a small obstacle course in your yard or living room using cones, pillows, or other markers. Practice moving quickly around the obstacles, focusing on your footwork and agility.

Tennis Ball Balance:

Place a tennis ball on a racket and try to walk a short distance without letting the ball fall off. This challenge helps improve your balance and coordination. You can increase the difficulty by walking further or trying to balance the ball on different types of surfaces.

Shadow Tennis:

Without a ball, practice your tennis swings and footwork in the air. Pretend you're hitting different types of shots like forehands, backhands, and serves. Focus on your form and technique, as if you were playing a real match.

Tennis Trivia Challenge:

Invite your family or friends to a tennis trivia game based on Rafael Nadal and general tennis knowledge. Ask each other questions and see who knows the most about the sport and Rafa's career!

CHAPTER 13:Rafael's Legacy

Rafael Nadal's Legacy and How He Inspires Future Generations

Rafael Nadal's legacy in tennis is not just about the impressive number of titles he's won but also about the values he embodies and the inspiration he provides to young players around the world. Here's a look at how

Rafa's legacy continues to influence and motivate future generations of tennis stars.

1. A Record-Breaking Career

Rafael Nadal's career is marked by a series of incredible achievements:

Grand Slam Titles: Nadal's record of 22 Grand Slam titles (as of 2024) highlights his dominance across different surfaces, particularly on clay. His achievements at the French Open, where he holds a record 14 titles, showcase his exceptional skill and consistency.

Diverse Surface Success: While he is renowned as the "King of Clay," Nadal has also proven his prowess on hard courts and grass, winning multiple Australian Open, Wimbledon, and US Open titles. This versatility demonstrates his all-around talent and adaptability.

2. Unmatched Work Ethic and Resilience

Rafa's approach to the game exemplifies dedication and hard work:

Relentless Training: Nadal's commitment to practice and preparation is legendary. His rigorous training routines and focus on improving every aspect of his game reflect his dedication to excellence.

Overcoming Injuries: Throughout his career, Rafa has faced numerous injuries, yet he has shown remarkable resilience. His ability to recover and come back stronger after setbacks is a powerful lesson in perseverance and determination.

3. Inspirational Sportsmanship

Nadal's conduct on and off the court serves as a model for sportsmanship:

Respect for Opponents: Rafa consistently shows respect and appreciation for his competitors, regardless of the outcome. His graciousness in both victory and defeat highlights the importance of treating others with kindness and respect.

Positive Attitude: His positive demeanor and mental toughness are inspirational. Nadal's ability to stay focused, calm, and composed under pressure teaches young athletes the value of maintaining a positive mindset.

4. Philanthropy and Giving Back

Rafa's contributions extend beyond tennis through his charitable work:

Rafael Nadal Foundation: The foundation supports education and sports programs for disadvantaged children. By providing resources and opportunities, Rafa helps empower young people to pursue their dreams, just as he did.

Community Involvement: Nadal's involvement in various charity events and initiatives demonstrates his commitment to giving back and making a difference in the lives of others.

5. Encouraging Future Generations

Rafael Nadal's influence on young players is profound:

Role Model: Rafa's journey from a young boy in Mallorca to a global tennis icon inspires young athletes to believe in their own potential. His story shows that with hard work, dedication, and passion, great achievements are possible.

Training and Mentorship: Nadal often shares his experiences and insights with aspiring players. His willingness to mentor and offer advice helps guide and motivate the next generation of tennis stars.

6. Legacy of Passion and Joy

Nadal's love for the game is evident in everything he does:

Joyful Play: Rafa's enthusiasm and passion for tennis shine through in his performances. His enjoyment of the sport reminds young players to have fun and find joy in their pursuit of excellence.

Inspiring Dedication: His unwavering dedication to his craft serves as a powerful example of what it means to follow one's passion with commitment and heart.

Rafael Nadal's legacy is defined by his extraordinary achievements, his dedication to the sport, and his positive impact on the world. As he continues to compete and inspire, his story will remain a beacon of motivation for future generations of tennis players and beyond. Whether on the court or through his charitable efforts, Rafa's influence will continue to shape and inspire the lives of many young athletes.

Rafael Nadal Trivia Quiz

Put your knowledge to the test with these fun questions about Rafael Nadal's life and career!

1. What year did Rafael Nadal win his first Grand Slam title?

A) 2003
B) 2005
C) 2007
D) 2009

2. How many times has Rafael Nadal won the French Open as of 2024?

A) 12

B) 14

C) 16

D) 18

3. What is Rafael Nadal's nickname that reflects his dominance on clay courts?

A) The King of Grass

B) The King of Clay

C) The Master of Hard Courts

D) The Spanish Sensation

4. Rafael Nadal was born on a Spanish island?

A) Ibiza

B) Tenerife

C) Mallorca

D) Gran Canaria

5. In which year did Rafael Nadal make his professional tennis debut?

A) 2001

B) 2002

C) 2003

D) 2004

6. What is the name of the charity foundation started by Rafael Nadal?

A) Rafa Nadal Foundation

B) Nadal's Heroes

C) Rafael's Relief Fund

D) Nadal Kids Foundation

7. Rafael Nadal has a famous rivalry with which other tennis legend?

A) Roger Federer

B) Novak Djokovic

C) Andy Murray

D) Pete Sampras

8. How many Olympic gold medals has Rafael Nadal won in tennis?

A) 1

B) 2

C) 3

D) 4

9. What other sport does Rafael Nadal enjoy playing besides tennis?

A) Basketball

B) Soccer (Football)

C) Baseball

D) Golf

10. Rafael Nadal's parents are named Sebastian and...?

A) Isabel

B) Maria

C) Laura

D) Ana

Answers:

B) 2005

B) 14

B) The King of Clay

C) Mallorca

B) 2002

A) Rafa Nadal Foundation

A) Roger Federer

A) 1

B) Soccer (Football)

A) Isabel

Have fun testing your knowledge of Rafael Nadal's incredible career and life!

CONCLUSION

Rafael Nadal, born on June 3, 1986, in Mallorca, Spain, is one of the most celebrated tennis players in history. His journey to becoming a tennis legend is marked by extraordinary achievements and inspiring dedication.

Early Life and Beginnings:

Rafa grew up on the beautiful island of Mallorca, where he first picked up a tennis racket at the age of three, inspired by his family's love for sports. His uncle, Toni Nadal, played a crucial role in his development, coaching him from a young age. Rafa's early years were filled with rigorous training and a passion for the game, setting the stage for his future success.

Rising Star:

Nadal turned professional in 2002 and quickly made a name for himself with his powerful game and relentless energy. In 2005, at just 19 years old, he won his first Grand Slam title at the French Open, marking the beginning of his dominance on clay courts. This victory earned him the nickname "King of Clay," reflecting his unmatched skill on this surface.

Major Achievements:

Throughout his career, Nadal has accumulated an impressive number of titles. He has won 22 Grand Slam titles, including a record 14 French Open titles. His versatility is evident in his successes across different surfaces, including hard courts and grass. Rafa's incredible work ethic, resilience, and ability to come back from injuries have defined his career.

Challenges and Resilience:

Nadal has faced several challenges, including injuries that have tested his determination. Despite these setbacks, he has shown remarkable resilience, often returning to the court stronger than before. His ability to overcome obstacles and continue performing at the highest level is a testament to his mental toughness and dedication.

Legacy and Inspiration:

Rafael Nadal's legacy extends beyond his tennis achievements. He is known for his sportsmanship, humility, and commitment to giving back through his charitable foundation, which supports education and sports programs for underprivileged children. His journey from a young boy in Mallorca to a global tennis icon serves as an inspiration to aspiring athletes around the world.

Advice and Impact:

Nadal's advice to young athletes emphasizes hard work, humility, and perseverance. He encourages everyone to follow their passions, stay dedicated, and always appreciate the support of others. His impact on the sport and his positive influence on future generations continue to inspire young players to strive for greatness.

Rafael Nadal's journey is a remarkable story of talent, hard work, and resilience, making him a true legend in the world of tennis and an inspiring figure for young athletes everywhere.

GLOSSARY

1. Grand Slam:

The four major tennis tournaments: the Australian Open, the French Open, Wimbledon, and the US Open. Winning all four in a single year is a significant achievement.

2. Clay Court:

A type of tennis court surface made of crushed clay. It's known for slowing down the ball and creating a high bounce, which Rafael Nadal excels on.

3. Rally:

A sequence of hits between players during a tennis match, starting with the serve and ending when the ball is out of play.

4. Serve:

The shot that starts each point in a tennis match. The player hits the ball from behind the baseline into the opponent's service box.

5. Backhand:

A tennis stroke where the player hits the ball with the back of the hand facing the net. It can be a one-handed or two-handed stroke.

6. Forehand:

A tennis stroke where the player hits the ball with the front of the hand facing the net. It's often the most powerful shot in a player's arsenal.

7. Topspin:

A type of spin put on the ball that makes it bounce higher and travel faster after hitting the ground. Nadal is known for his heavy topspin shots.

8. Net:

The barrier that divides the two sides of the tennis court. Players must hit the ball over the net to their opponent's side.

9. Footwork:

The way a player moves their feet to position themselves correctly for shots. Good footwork is essential for reaching and hitting the ball effectively.

10. Tiebreaker:

A special game played when the score in a set is tied at 6-6. The first player to reach 7 points wins the tiebreaker and the set.

11. Foundation:

A charitable organization set up to support causes and help those in need. Rafael Nadal's foundation focuses on education and sports for disadvantaged children.

12. Sportsmanship:

The way players conduct themselves during a game, including respect for opponents, fairness, and graciousness in winning or losing.

13. Injury Recovery:

The process of healing and returning to play after an injury. It involves rest, treatment, and rehabilitation to regain full strength and fitness.

14. Philanthropy:

The act of giving money or resources to help others, often through charities or foundations. Nadal's philanthropy includes supporting various causes through his foundation.

15. Versatility:

The ability to perform well on different surfaces or in various situations. Nadal's success on clay, grass, and hard courts shows his versatility as a player.

Made in United States
Orlando, FL
02 October 2024

52288617R00039